Weather

Words by Herta S. Breiter

formerly Research Chemist
University of Illinois

Raintree Childrens Books

Milwaukee • Toronto • Melbourne • London

Library of Congress Number: 77-27239

4   5   6   7   8   9   0   82   81   80

Printed and bound in the United States of America.

Library of Congress Cataloging in Publication Data

Breiter, Herta S.
    Weather.

    (Read about)
    Bibliography: p.
    Includes index.
    SUMMARY: An introduction to weather discussing such
concepts as evaporation and condensation and the natural
occurrence of rain, snow, thunderstorms, and hurricanes.
    1.   Weather — Juvenile literature.   2.   Meteorology —
Juvenile literature.   [1.   Weather.   2.   Meteorology]
I.   Title.
QC981.3.M67   551.5   77-27239
ISBN 0-8393-0079-4 lib. bdg.

Weather

There is air all around the earth. This layer of air is called the atmosphere. Astronauts looked at the earth from space and saw the atmosphere as a blue haze. But there is no haze around the moon. The moon has no atmosphere.

The atmosphere is very important. It gives us the air we breathe. It keeps us from getting too much heat from the sun. It keeps the earth warm at night.

Sometimes the air is warm. Sometimes it is cold. Sometimes the air is damp. Sometimes it is dry. These are some of the changes we call weather.

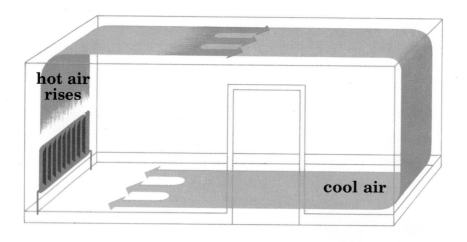

hot air rises

cool air

    If you hold your hands over a radiator, you can feel hot air that is rising from it. The air is made hot by the radiator. The hot air expands. It rises because it is lighter than the cold air around it. The cold air pushes on the warmer air. As the hot air rises, cooler air moves in to take its place. The same kind of movement happens in the atmosphere when the air becomes warm.

Heat from the sun warms the land. Land near the equator gets the hottest. The land then warms the air. The heated air rises. As it rises, it cools. Finally, the cool air sinks and spreads over the land. This moving air is wind.

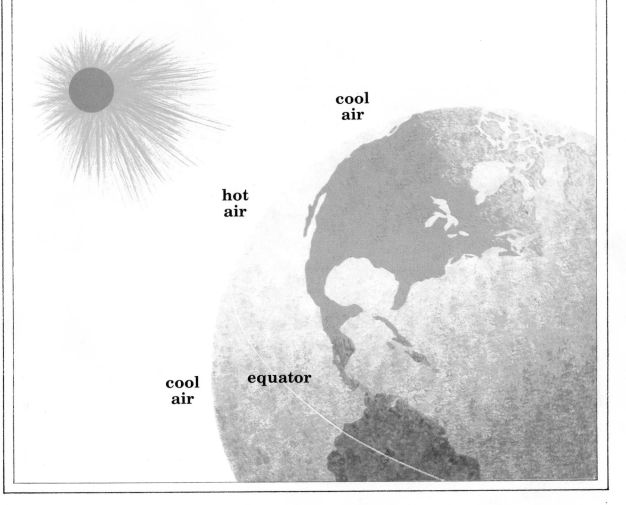

cool air

hot air

cool air

equator

force 1   force 2   force 3

A wind may be weak, or it may be strong. Weather scientists use numbers to describe the force of winds. The numbers make up a scale from one to twelve. The pictures show how this scale works.

force 7   force 8   force 9

force 4

force 5

force 6

At Force 1, the wind is moving at only a few miles an hour. You can hardly feel it. But in a Force 10 gale, the wind may be traveling at 55 miles per hour (88.5 kilometers per hour). It will uproot trees and damage houses.

force 10

force 11

force 12

The atmosphere can hold water. This water is in the form of a gas called water vapor. When liquid water is heated, it disappears. The heat changes the water into water vapor. The water disappears into the atmosphere. This is called evaporation.

Evaporation happens all the time. The sun heats the water in oceans, rivers, and lakes. This makes the water evaporate into the air.

evaporation

condensation

dew

Warm air can hold more water vapor than cold air can. When warm air gets colder, some of its vapor turns back into water. This is called condensation. If you put a glass of ice water in a warm room, water vapor from the air will condense on the cold glass. Dew is formed in this way. It is condensed vapor. Dew condenses from air that has cooled. The air was too cold to hold the water vapor.

Condensation also causes fog. Fog forms when warm, moist air near the ground is cooled. The water vapor condenses into millions of tiny drops of water. The drops of water stay in the air. This is called fog. Fog often forms on clear, cold nights. The land cools very quickly. The air soon gets cold, and water vapor condenses as fog.

land fog

Fog forms at sea too. It often forms
when a stream of cold water meets warmer
water. The air moving over the warm water
is warm and full of water vapor. When this
warm, moist air passes over the cold
stream, it is quickly cooled. As its water
vapor condenses, fog forms.

sea fog

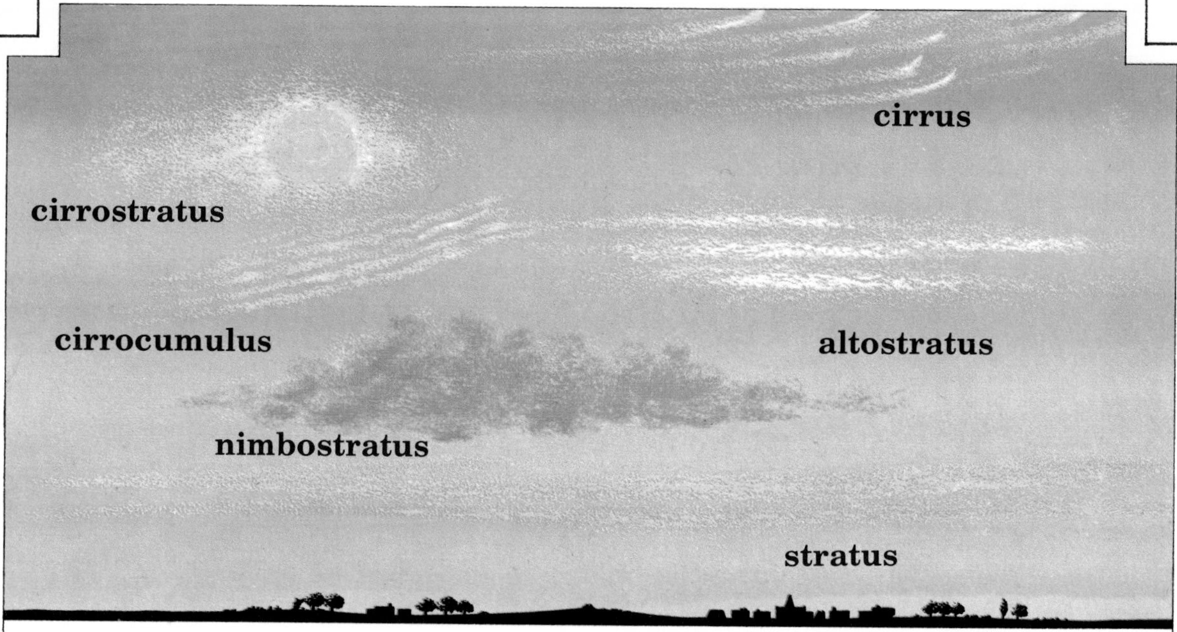

cirrus

cirrostratus

cirrocumulus

altostratus

nimbostratus

stratus

Condensation also happens in the sky. It makes clouds. Some clouds are made up of millions of tiny drops of water. These clouds are like fog.

If it is very cold, the clouds are made of ice crystals instead of water droplets.

There are many different kinds of clouds.

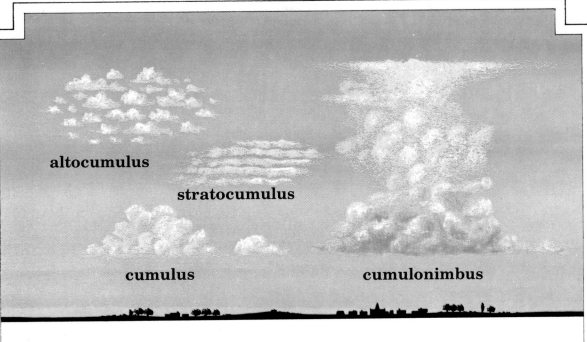

Some clouds look like gray blankets across the sky. These are called stratus clouds. Cirrus clouds are little wisps. You can see them high in the sky. They are made of ice crystals. Cumulus clouds look like puffs of cotton. But some cumulus clouds grow into big, dark thunderclouds. They are called cumulonimbus clouds.

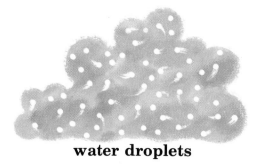
water droplets

Rain clouds are made of tiny water droplets. At first, the droplets are so small and light that they stay up in the air.

drops grow bigger

The droplets are always moving. When they bump into each other, they join together. They grow larger.

rain falls

They become heavy. They may become too heavy to hang in the air. Then they fall to the ground as rain.

Clouds are formed when air rises and cools. As a cloud rises, it gets cooler. It may condense as rain.

Suppose air is pushed over high land. This air will cool as it rises. The higher it rises, the cooler it becomes. Suddenly its water vapor condenses to form a cloud. The water droplets in the cloud grow bigger and bigger. Then they fall as rain. Look at the picture and see why it rains a lot in the mountains.

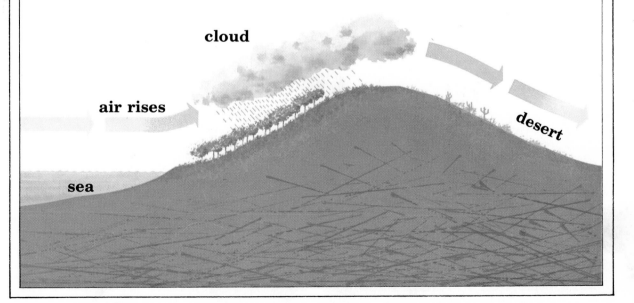

snow crystals

Sometimes clouds are made of ice instead of water droplets. The tiny ice crystals grow bigger as more water vapor condenses on them. They may become so heavy that they fall to earth. If the air below is very cold, the crystals fall as snow. If the air is warm, they melt and fall as rain.

frost

    Snow crystals always have six sides. But each snow crystal has a different pattern.

    Frost can make beautiful patterns too. You can see these patterns on windows on a very cold night. Frost is caused by water vapor condensing on a very cold surface. Frost is sometimes called frozen dew.

Great masses of cold air and warm air move through the atmosphere all the time. Cold high-pressure masses push on warmer low-pressure masses and move them. When a mass of warm air meets a mass of cold air, the weather changes. The line where they meet is called a front.

When a mass of warm air catches up with a mass of cold air, a warm front forms.

cold front

cold air

warm air

The warm air is lighter than the cold air. It rises slowly over the cold air. As it rises, clouds form and rain falls.

When a mass of cold air catches up with a mass of warm air, a cold front forms. The cold air moves under the warm air and pushes it up. Clouds form, and often heavy rain falls. There may even be thunderstorms.

Thunderstorms happen when hot, moist air rises fast and then cools quickly. Dark clouds form and either big drops of rain or hail falls. Lightning flashes, and there is thunder. Lightning is a big electric spark.

Thunder is the noise made when air expands suddenly. The heat of the lightning expands the air.

Hail forms from freezing raindrops as they go up and down in a thundercloud. As they go up, they freeze. As they come down, they pick up layers of water and freeze again. When the hailstones get heavy, they fall to earth.

hailstones cut in half

Hurricanes are violent storms. They begin over warm seas, where the air is hot and moist. The air circles around and around as it rises. It goes faster and faster and faster. Soon the wind is roaring, and much rain beats down. Hurricanes can cause a lot of damage when they reach the land.

hurricane

The center of a hurricane is called the eye. It is very calm. This eye can be tracked from airplanes or by radar. Hurricanes can be photographed by satellites traveling around the earth. Weather scientists warn people when one is coming.

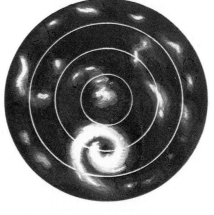

hurricane on radar screen

A tornado is another kind of violent storm. It is a great column of whirling air. It reaches from the ground right up to the clouds. Tornadoes are very dangerous.

tornado

Tornadoes begin over very hot land. Cold air flows in, and the hot air rises very fast and whirls around and around. As the tornado moves, it sucks up anything in its path. Dust, fences, roofs, and even cars are lifted high into the air and dropped back to earth. Tornadoes do not last very long.

Our weather changes from day to day. But the kind of weather we have from year to year stays about the same. The year-to-year weather is called the climate. Different parts of the world have different climates. Some are hot. Some are cold. Some are wet. Some are dry.

Lands near the equator are hot all the time. Near the north and south poles, the weather is very cold all the time. Between the equator and the poles, lands have warm or hot summers. And they have cool or cold winters. In the wettest lands, it rains every day. In some of the driest lands, it may not rain for many years.

north pole

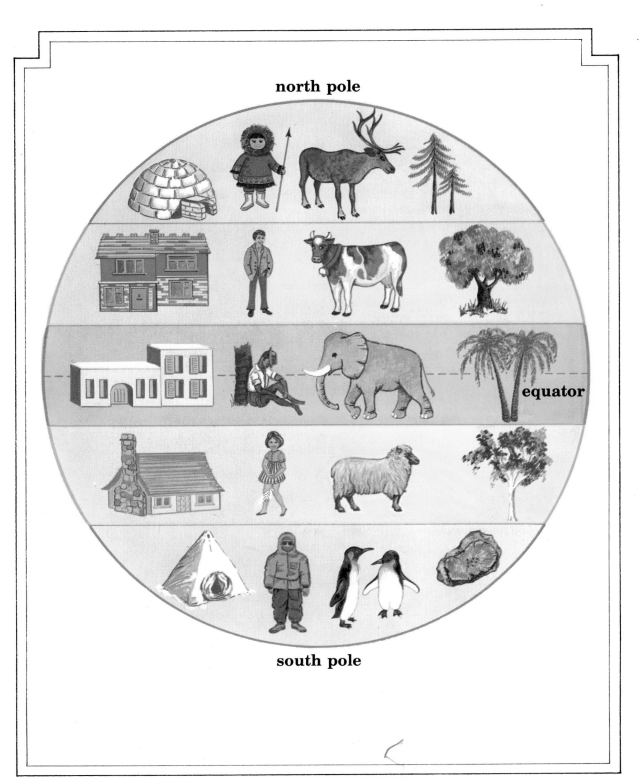

equator

south pole

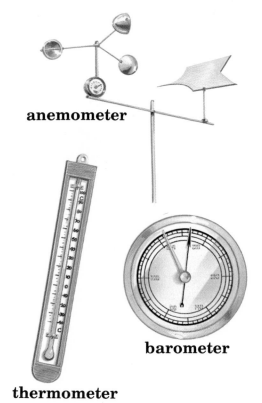

anemometer

thermometer

barometer

rain gauge

Many different instruments are used to measure the weather.

An anemometer measures the speed of the wind. It has cups that catch the wind and spin around. The stronger the wind, the faster the cups spin.

A thermometer measures how hot or cold the air is. A barometer measures the pressure of the air. If its reading is getting lower, a low-pressure air mass is coming. Maybe even a storm.

Rainfall is measured with a rain gauge. The rain falls into a funnel and drips into a tube. The amount of water in the tube shows how much rain has fallen that day.

We can find out about the weather high in the sky with radiosondes. These are radio instruments that are carried by balloons. Each radiosonde sends information back to a weather station on earth.

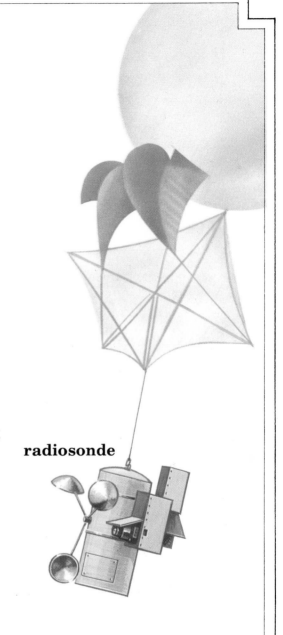

radiosonde

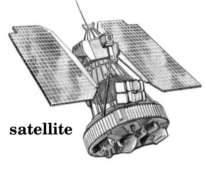

satellite

tracking station

photograph of hurricane

People who study the weather are called meteorologists. A meteorologist tries to tell us what the weather will be like. That is called forecasting.

Meteorologists use weather instruments to help make forecasts. They also learn from other weather stations what the weather is like there.

They may even use pictures of clouds taken by weather satellites.

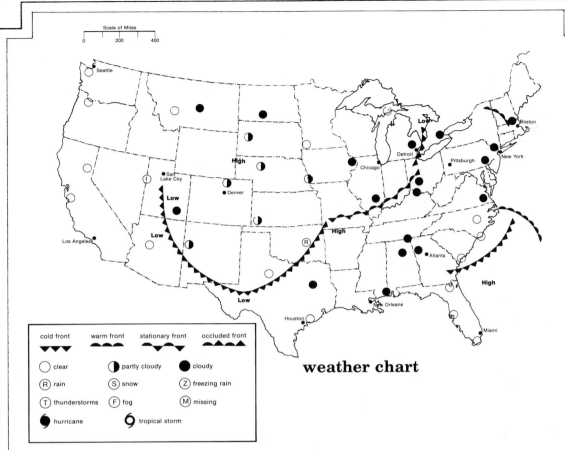

weather chart

Legend:

Scale of Miles
0 200 400

cold front ▼▼▼ warm front ◠◠◠ stationary front ◠▼◠▼ occluded front ▲▲▲

○ clear ◑ partly cloudy ● cloudy

Ⓡ rain Ⓢ snow Ⓩ freezing rain

Ⓣ thunderstorms Ⓕ fog Ⓜ missing

🌀 hurricane 🌀 tropical storm

   Meteorologists make charts to show
what the weather is like. They use special
symbols. There is a symbol for every kind
of weather. The symbols show rain, snow,
fog, cold or warm fronts, clouds, and
wind speed. By looking at the chart, the
meteorologist can forecast what the
weather will be like tomorrow.

Average Yearly Rainfall of the World

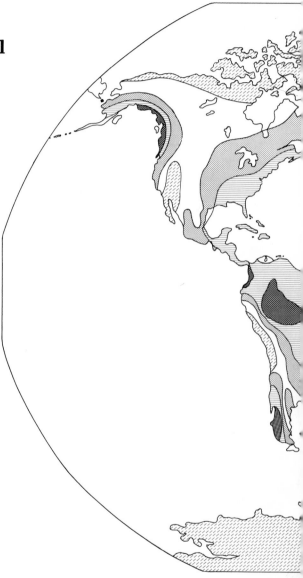

- ■ over 80 in. (203 cm)
- 40-80 in. (102-203 cm)
- 20-40 in. (51-102 cm)
- 10-20 in. (25-51 cm)
- under 10 in. (25 cm)

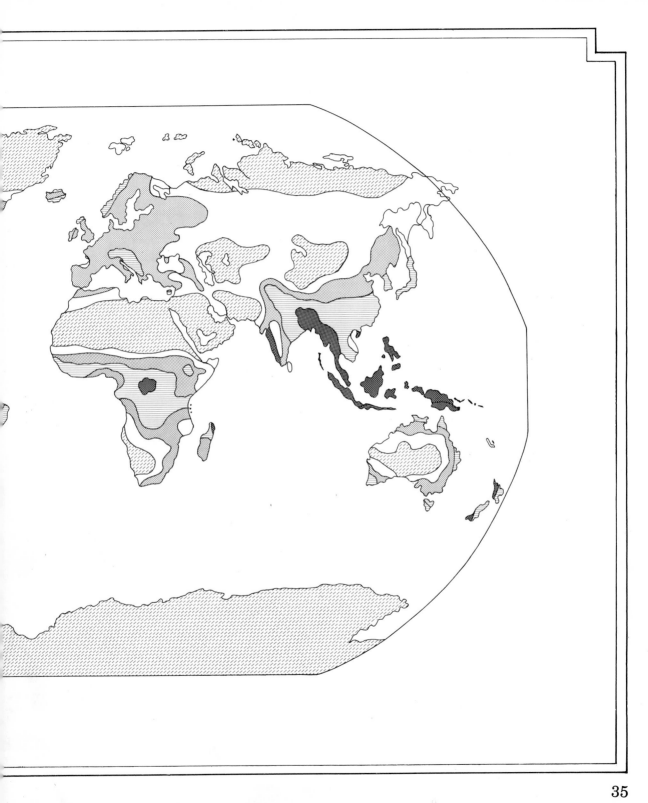

The Metric System

In the United States, things are measured in inches, pounds, quarts, and so on. Most countries of the world use centimeters, kilograms, and liters for these things. The United States uses the American system to measure things. Most other countries use the metric system. By 1985, the United States will be using the metric system, too.

In some books, you will see two systems of measurement. For example, you might see a sentence like this: "That bicycle wheel is 27 inches (69 centimeters) across." When all countries have changed to the metric system, inches will not be used any more. But until then, you may sometimes have to change measurements from one system to the other. The chart on the next page will help you.

All you have to do is multiply the unit of measurement in Column 1 by the number in Column 2. That gives you the unit in Column 3.

Suppose you want to change 5 inches to centimeters. First, find inches in Column 1. Next, multiply 5 times 2.54. You get 12.7. So, 5 inches is 12.7 centimeters.

Column 1	Column 2	Column 3
THIS UNIT OF MEASUREMENT	TIMES THIS NUMBER	GIVES THIS UNIT OF MEASUREMENT
inches	2.54	centimeters
feet	30.	centimeters
feet	.3	meters
yards	.9	meters
miles	1.6	kilometers
ounces	28.	grams
pounds	.45	kilograms
fluid ounces	.03	liters
pints	.47	liters
quarts	.95	liters
gallons	3.8	liters
centimeters	.4	inches
meters	1.1	yards
kilometers	.6	miles
grams	.035	ounces
kilograms	2.2	pounds
liters	33.8	fluid ounces
liters	2.1	pints
liters	1.06	quarts
liters	.26	gallons

Where to Read About Weather

Pronunciation Key

a	a as in **cat, bad**
$\bar{\text{a}}$	a as in **able**, ai as in **train**, ay as in **play**
ä	a as in **father, car**, o as in **cot**
e	e as in **bend, yet**
$\bar{\text{e}}$	e as in **me**, ee as in **feel**, ea as in **beat**, ie as in **piece**, y as in **heavy**
i	i as in **in, pig**, e as in **pocket**
ī	i as in **ice, time**, ie as in **tie**, y as in **my**
o	o as in **top**, a as in **watch**
ō	o as in **old**, oa as in **goat**, ow as in **slow**, oe as in **toe**
ô	o as in **cloth**, au as in **caught**, aw as in **paw**, a as in **all**
oo	oo as in **good**, u as in **put**
$\overline{\text{oo}}$	oo as in **tool**, ue as in **blue**
oi	oi as in **oil**, oy as in **toy**
ou	ou as in **out**, ow as in **plow**
u	u as in **up, gun**, o as in **other**
ur	ur as in **fur**, er as in **person**, ir as in **bird**, or as in **work**
y$\overline{\text{oo}}$	u as in **use**, ew as in **few**
ə	a as in **again**, e as in **broken**, i as in **pencil**, o as in **attention**, u as in **surprise**
ch	ch as in **such**
ng	ng as in **sing**
sh	sh as in **shell, wish**
th	th as in **three, bath**
<u>th</u>	th as in **that, together**

GLOSSARY

These words are defined the way they are used in this book

air (er) the layer of gases that is all around the earth

anemometer (an ə mäm′ ə tər) a device that measures the speed of the wind

atmosphere (at′ məs fēr) the air that is all around the earth

barometer (bə räm′ ə tər) a device that measures the pressure of the air

cirrus (sir′ əs) a cloud that looks like a wisp

climate (klī′ mət) the year-to-year weather in different parts of the world

cold front (kōld frunt) the front that forms when a mass of cold air catches up with a mass of warm air

condensation (kän′ dən sā′ shən) the water that forms when water vapor is cooled

41

cumulonimbus (kyōo′ myə lō nim′ bəs) a large black cloud; also called a thundercloud

cumulus (kyōo′ myə ləs) a cloud that looks like a puff of cotton

dew (dōo) the water that forms on grass and some other things when the air is too cold to hold all the water vapor

droplet (dräp′ lət) a small drop

equator (ē kwāt′ ər) an imaginary line that goes around the middle of the earth

evaporation (ē vap′ ə rā′ shən) when water is heated and disappears into the air it is called evaporation

fog (fôg) condensation formed near the ground when water vapor changes into millions of tiny droplets of water

forecast (fôr′ kast′) to try to tell what the weather will be like

front (frunt) the line where two different air masses meet

frost (frôst) the ice patterns that form on things when it is very cold outside

gale (gāl) wind that is traveling about 50 miles per hour (80.5 kilometers per hour)

hail (hāl) frozen raindrops

hurricane (hur′ ə kān) a violent storm made up of air traveling very rapidly in circles

ice crystal (īs′ kris′ təl) a small, clear piece of ice

lightning (līt′ ning) a flash of light in the sky; a big electric spark

meteorologist (mē′ tē ər äl′ ə jist) a person who studies the weather

radar (rā′ dar) a device that uses radio waves to find objects in the sky

radiator (rā′ dē ā′ tər) a device that gives off heat and is used to warm a room

radiosonde (rā′ dē ō sänd′) an instrument carried on a balloon that sends information to earth about weather high in the sky

rain (rān) drops of water that fall from clouds

rain gauge (rān gāj) a device that measures the amount of rain that falls

satellite (sat′ əl īt) an object made by humans that is orbiting some body in space

snow (snō) ice crystals that fall from clouds

space (spās) the part of the sky that is beyond the atmosphere

stratus cloud (strāt′ əs kloud′) the kind of cloud that looks like a blanket

thermometer (thər mäm′ ə tər) a device that measures how hot or cold the air is

thunder (thun′ dər) the noise made when air expands suddenly

tornado (tôr nā′ dō) a violent storm in the form of a large column of whirling air

warm front (wôrm frunt) the front that forms when a mass of warm air catches up with a mass of cold air

water vapor (wô′ tər vā′ pər) the gas
  that is formed by heating water
weather (we<u>th</u>′ ər) conditions in the
  atmosphere, such as cold, hot, damp, dry
wind (wind) moving air

Bibliography

Boesen, Victor. *Doing Something About the Weather.* New York: G. P. Putnam's Sons, 1975.

Bova, Ben. *Weather Changes Man.* Reading, Mass.: Addison-Wesley Publishing Co., 1974.

Forsdyke, A. G. *Weather and Weather Forecasting.* New York: Grosset and Dunlap, Inc., 1970.

Iger, Eve M. *Weather on the Move.* Reading, Mass.: Addison-Wesley Publishing Co., 1970.

Kaufman, John. *Winds and Weather.* New York: William Morrow and Co., 1971.

Thompson, Phillip D. *Weather.* New York: Time-Life Books, 1973.

Weiss, Malcolm. *Storms.* New York: Julian Messner, 1973.

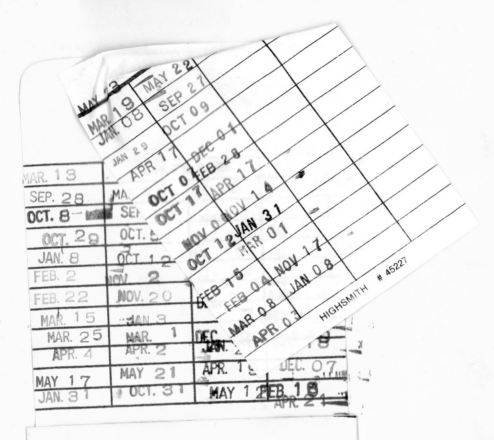